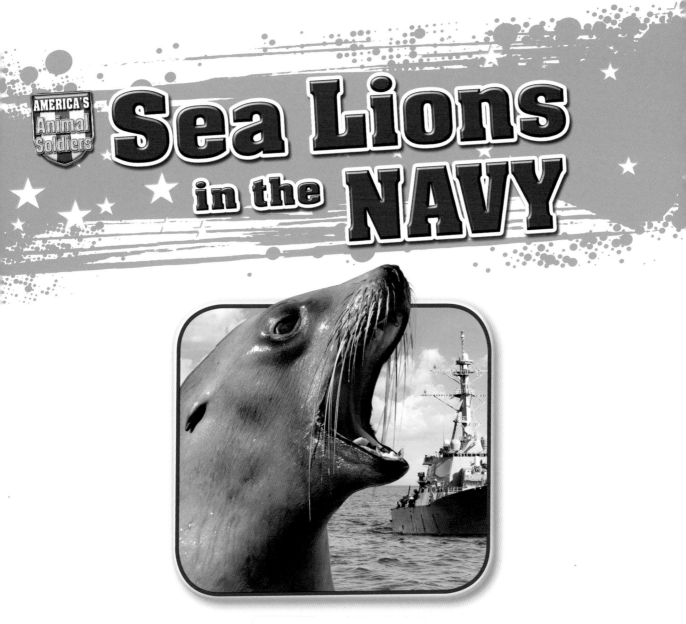

# Sea Lions in the NAVY

AMERICA'S Animal Soldiers

3 1389 02114 3250

**by Meish Goldish**

Consultant: Sam Ridgway DVM, PhD, DACZM
President, National Marine Mammal Foundation
San Diego, California

BEARPORT PUBLISHING

New York, New York

## Credits

Cover and Title Page, © Herbert Kehrer/imagebroker/AGE Fotostock and © SpotX/iStock photo; 4, Courtesy of The National Marine Mammal Foundation; 5, © United States Navy/Barcroft Media/Fame Pictures, Inc; 6, © AP Photo/Mindaugas Kulbis; 7, © Norbert Wu/Minden Pictures/SuperStock; 8, © U.S. Navy/Photographer's Mate 2nd Class Bob Houlihan; 9, Courtesy of The National Marine Mammal Foundation; 10L, © Louise Murray/AGE Fotostock; 10R, Courtesy of The National Marine Mammal Foundation; 11L, Courtesy of The National Marine Mammal Foundation; 11R, © Stefan Huwiler/ Imagebroker/AGE Fotostock; 12, © Larsen & Talbert; 13, Courtesy of The National Marine Mammal Foundation; 14, © U.S. Navy/ Photographer's Mate First Class Brien Aho; 16, © U.S. Navy/Photographer's Mate 2nd Class Andrew McKaskle; 17, Courtesy of The National Marine Mammal Foundation; 18, Courtesy of The National Marine Mammal Foundation; 19T, Courtesy of The National Marine Mammal Foundation; 19B, © Louise Murray/AGE Fotostock; 20-21, © U.S. Navy/ Photographer's Mate First Class Brien Aho; 22, © Charles Hood/ Oceans Image/Photoshot; 23, © visceralimage/Shutterstock.

Publisher: Kenn Goin
Editorial Director: Adam Siegel
Creative Director: Spencer Brinker
Design: Debrah Kaiser
Photo Researcher: James O'Connor

*Library of Congress Cataloging-in-Publication Data*

Goldish, Meish.
  Sea lions in the Navy / by Meish Goldish.
     p. cm. — (America's animal soliders)
  Includes bibliographical references and index.
  ISBN-13: 978-1-61772-450-3 (library binding)
  ISBN-10: 1-61772-450-5 (library binding)
 1.  Sea lions—War use—Juvenile literature. 2.  United States. Navy—History—21st century—Juvenile literature.  I. Title.
  UH100.5.S43G65 2012
  599.79'75—dc23
                          2011033527

For more information, write to Bearport Publishing Company, Inc., 45 West 21st Street, Suite 3B, New York, New York 10010. Printed in the United States of America in North Mankato, Minnesota.

10 9 8 7 6 5 4 3 2 1

# CONTENTS

# Bomb in the Water

Gremlin slid off his **raft** and dove deep into the water. Moving quickly, the expert swimmer soon spotted what he was looking for—a sea mine that had been placed on the ocean floor. Without wasting a second, he quickly attached a **clamp** to the mine. Workers on the raft held one end of a rope that had been tied to the clamp. They were now able to safely pull the bomb out of the water.

A sea mine is a kind of bomb placed in the water by swimmers who are trying to blow up enemy ships and submarines.

Gremlin holds a clamp in his mouth as he approaches a mine. The mines used to train sea lions are placed as deep as 1,000 feet (305 m) in the water.

It had taken Gremlin just a few minutes to do his job. Amazingly, Gremlin isn't even a human—he's a sea lion! He was trained by the U.S. **Navy** to protect American sailors and ships from danger. The mine that Gremlin found wasn't real. It was actually part of a Navy **exercise** to test his skills.

Gremlin is about to enter the water.

# Why Sea Lions?

Gremlin is one of about 30 California sea lions that work for the U.S. Navy. They are trained, along with **bottlenose dolphins**, to **patrol** sea and **coastal** waters. The animals are part of the Navy **Marine Mammal** Program, based in San Diego, California.

Why does the Navy sometimes use sea lions instead of people to help guard the water? One of the main reasons is the animals' speed. Sea lions swim much faster than humans do. In addition, their long, narrow bodies let them weave easily through tight spaces. Sea lions also see five times better than humans in the deep, dark ocean. They hear better, too. They can easily pick up the sound of something moving far away in the water.

A sea lion can swim at a speed of up to 25 miles per hour (40 kph). That's about five times faster than a swimmer in an Olympic race.

A sea lion can make many deep dives without getting tired or suffering from a dangerous type of pain called "the **bends**," which human divers often experience.

# Partners with People

Sea lions are more skillful in the water than humans are. However, they still work together with people on the job. For example, to search an area for mines, a sea lion starts out riding in a Navy boat with two or three human **handlers**. Sometimes the handlers put a **harness** and leash on the animal to track it after it disappears into the water.

This sea lion wears a yellow harness. He is getting back on his boat after performing his job.

Once the sea lion has located a mine, it attaches a clamp. The sea lion tugs on it to make sure the connection is good. Then the animal returns to the boat. The handlers are now able to reel in the mine. A human-and-animal team works well together. It might take weeks for a team made up of only human divers to locate a mine. However, sea lions working with people can find a mine in a matter of minutes.

These photos show a sea lion holding a clamp in its mouth, attaching it to a sea mine, and a mine after it has been safely lifted out of the ocean.

Sea mines come in different shapes and sizes. Navy trainers teach sea lions to recognize the different kinds.

# On the Job

California sea lions do more than just locate mines. They are also trained to find other things underwater, such as Navy equipment that has been dropped into the ocean by a plane. The sea lions can also recover lost items such as **drones**—planes without pilots—that have crashed and sunk into the sea.

A sea lion recovers a drone.

Sea lions are very smart, so it is easy to train them to do many different kinds of jobs.

A trained sea lion can even capture an enemy in the water. It sneaks up on the person by swimming quickly and quietly. When it gets close enough, the animal snaps a leg cuff—similar to a handcuff—around the enemy's leg. The leg cuff is attached to a rope so that Navy workers can pull the person from the water to learn who he or she is. Sea lions are so quick that they can attach a clamp to a swimmer's leg before he or she knows what has happened.

Unlike some other kinds of seals, sea lions can use their flippers to walk on land.

Sea lions can chase swimmers out of the water and then follow them. They move on land by using their four flippers.

# Meet a Trainer

California sea lions can perform many jobs in the water. However, it takes a good trainer to teach them what to do. Craig Swepston has worked with the Navy Marine Mammal Program for more than 20 years. He thinks of the sea lions he trains as "underwater guard dogs."

Craig works with Joe, a sea lion he is training.

Craig works in the waters off San Diego. His 33-foot-long (10-m-long) boat can hold up to four sea lions. It also carries training equipment for the animals, including hooks, ropes, harnesses, and fake sea mines. When a sea lion performs a **task** correctly, Craig rewards the animal with a handful of small fish.

A sea lion is never punished if it performs poorly in the water. Instead, the trainer ignores the wrong action and works to correct it through more practice and by rewarding only correct behavior.

These Navy sea lions are ready to go to work in San Francisco Bay.

# Branching Out

The Navy Marine Mammal Program began in 1960, long before Craig Swepston signed on as a trainer. At first, the Navy trained only dolphins. However, it soon began to work with sea lions as well. Dolphins served between 1970 and 1971 during the Vietnam War (1957–1975). The success of these intelligent sea mammals led the Navy to increase their work with sea lions, starting in 1972.

The Navy's dolphins and sea lions can be **deployed** anywhere in the world within 72 hours. They are transported by ships, helicopters, and airplanes.

Zak is a sea lion that is trained to spot enemy divers. Like all sea lions, his sharp sense of hearing and his keen night vision help him locate swimmers—even in the middle of the night.

In the 2000s, sea lions and dolphins served in the **Persian Gulf**. They were flown from San Diego on U.S. Air Force transport planes. The sea lions helped guard Navy boats and submarines. They swam around **piers** looking for **terrorists** who might try to blow up ships by attaching **explosives** to them. If a sea lion found an enemy diver, the animal would quickly attach a cuff to the diver's leg so that he could be pulled out of the water.

■ Where Navy marine mammals have been deployed

The purple parts of this map show the places where animals from the Navy Marine Mammal Program have served.

# Safety First

The U.S. Navy has been training marine mammals for more than 50 years. Not everyone, however, has been pleased with the program. Some people felt it was cruel to use sea lions and dolphins for dangerous **security** work. To address their concerns, in 1988 and 1990 the **Marine Mammal Commission**—an organization created by the U.S. government—**investigated** the ways the Navy animals were treated. The commission found that the sea lions and dolphins were treated very well and were never placed in risky or dangerous situations.

The Navy makes sure that sea lions are safely out of the way when workers reel in or handle a mine.

Sea lions that work for the Navy program are in less danger from their work than sea lions that live in the wild—many of which may suffer from disease, are killed and eaten by sharks, or are fed unsafe food by people.

Most important, none of the animals in the Marine Mammal Program have ever been **injured** or killed because of their work. In addition, the sea lions receive excellent medical care from Navy **veterinarians**. Off duty, the sea lions swim in safe, enclosed areas where they are fed a steady diet of fish and squid. Because the sea lions are treated so well, it is very rare that any of them ever swim away to live on their own, even though they often swim freely in the open sea.

A veterinarian (left) examines a sea lion to make sure it is healthy.

# Student Aid

The Navy wants the **public** to take an interest in its Marine Mammal Program. As a result, students from around the country are invited to serve as **interns** every year. In one program, college students feed and clean the sea lions and care for their equipment. They also attend classes and go on field trips. Students put in 40 hours a week for 16 weeks.

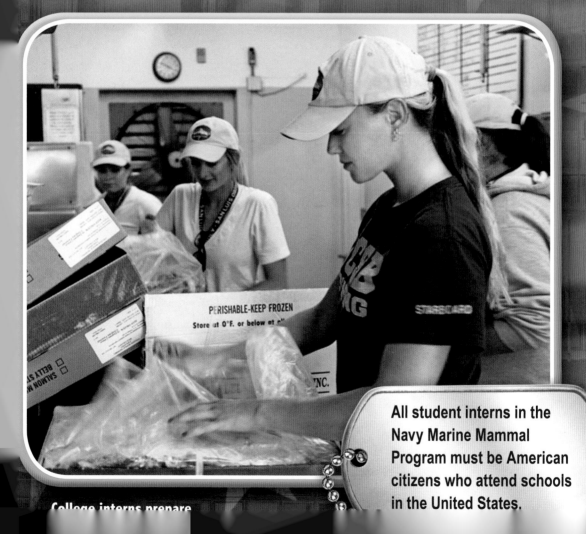

College interns prepare

All student interns in the Navy Marine Mammal Program must be American citizens who attend schools in the United States.

The second program is for veterinary students. They help to provide medical care for the animals. They must also complete a project in marine mammal medicine during their stay. The program lasts four to six weeks. Only four students are chosen each year to take part.

A student washes the deck by the sea lions' swimming area.

Students come to this training area in San Diego to help care for the dolphins and sea lions in the Navy Marine Mammal Program.

NO Photography & Recording Devices Permitted

CODE 35 AUTHORIZED PERSONS — ONLY

KEEP OUT. RESTRICTED AREA

# The Future for Sea Lions

For more than 45 years, California sea lions have helped the U.S. Navy. Now, other countries are interested in using sea lions and other marine mammals in the war against terror. Recently, the U.S. Navy displayed the animals' amazing abilities for members of the North Atlantic Treaty Organization (NATO).

NATO is made up of 28 countries around the world, including the United States, Canada, Italy, France, Poland, and Germany. They work together to achieve peace and security.

Even with the program's success, the Navy believes that it will someday be able to rely on underwater machines instead of sea lions to protect and patrol piers and oceans. However, at the moment there are still no machines that can be built to match these animals' excellent underwater abilities. So for now, sea lions will remain on duty. They will continue to play an important role in keeping America's waters safe.

# More About
# California Sea Lions

The California sea lion is really a kind of seal. The name *sea lion* comes from the roaring sound that a male sometimes makes. Altogether, there are six kinds of sea lions living in the world's oceans.

Although some California sea lions work for the U.S. Navy, most of these mammals live in the wild. Here is some more information about them.

A male sea lion roaring

| Weight | 150–1,000 pounds (68–454 kg) |
|---|---|
| Length | 5–8 feet (1.5–2.4 m) |
| Life Span | 20–25 years |
| Average Speed | 20 miles per hour (32 kph), but can reach up to 25 miles per hour (40 kph) in brief spurts |
| Food | fish, octopuses, squid |
| Habitat | from British Columbia to Baja California in Mexico |
| Predators | killer whales, sharks |

**bends** (BENDZ) a dangerous and painful condition in which gas bubbles form in a person's blood and muscles; they can occur if a diver returns to the water's surface too quickly

**bottlenose dolphins** (BOT-uhl-*nohz* DOL-finz) a type of sea mammal with a snout that looks like a beak; they are known for being very smart

**clamp** (KLAMP) a tool for holding things tightly together

**coastal** (KOHST-uhl) having to do with land that runs along an ocean

**deployed** (di-PLOYD) sent to an area for a specific purpose

**drones** (DROHNZ) airplanes without pilots that are flown by remote control

**exercise** (EK-sur-*syez*) an activity that is used for training

**explosives** (ek-SPLOH-sivz) substances that can blow things up

**handlers** (HAND-lurz) people who work with and train animals

**harness** (HAR-niss) a set of straps that is attached to a leash and that an animal wears so a person can control its movements

**injured** (IN-jurd) hurt

**interns** (IN-turnz) people who learn a skill or job by working with experts in that field

**investigated** (in-VESS-tuh-*gayt*-id) searched for information to find out about something

**marine mammal** (muh-REEN MAM-uhl) a warm-blooded animal that lives in the ocean, has hair or fur on its skin, and drinks its mother's milk as a baby

**Marine Mammal Commission** (muh-REEN MAM-uhl kuh-MISH-uhn) an organization that was created by the U.S. government in 1972 for the protection and conservation of marine mammals

**Navy** (NAY-vee) a branch of the armed forces that is responsible for military operations on the seas

**patrol** (puh-TROHL) to travel around an area to protect it

**Persian Gulf** (PUR-zhuhn GUHLF) a body of water in southwestern Asia that is surrounded by several countries, including Saudi Arabia, Iran, and Iraq

**piers** (PEERZ) structures built over water that are used as walkways or landing places for boats

**public** (PUHB-lik) people in a community

**raft** (RAFT) a rubber or wooden craft with a flat bottom that travels on water

**security** (si-KYOOR-uh-tee) safety

**task** (TASK) a job or duty

**terrorists** (TER-ur-ists) individuals or groups that use violence and terror to get what they want

**veterinarians** (*vet*-ur-uh-NAIR-ee-uhnz) doctors who try to prevent animals from getting injured or coming down with diseases and who treat sick or injured animals

# Index

# Bibliography

**Cleave, Andrew.** *Seals & Sea Lions*. New York: New Line (2005).

**Kistler, John M.** *Animals in the Military: From Hannibal's Elephants to the Dolphins of the U.S. Navy*. Santa Barbara, CA: ABC-CLIO (2011).

**Le Chêne, Evelyn.** *Silent Heroes: The Bravery and Devotion of Animals in War*. London: Souvenir Press (2009).

**U.S. Navy Marine Mammal Program** (www.public.navy.mil/spawar/Pacific/71500/Pages/default.aspx)

# Read More

**Fetty, Margaret.** *Sea Lions (Smart Animals!)*. New York: Bearport (2007).

**Goldish, Meish.** *Dolphins in the Navy (America's Animal Soldiers)*. New York: Bearport (2012).

**Grayson, Robert.** *Military (Working Animals)*. Tarrytown, NY: Marshall Cavendish Benchmark (2011).

**Murray, Julie.** *Military Animals (Going to Work)*. Edina, MN: ABDO (2009).

# Learn More Online

To learn more about sea lions in the U.S. Navy, visit
**www.bearportpublishing.com/AmericasAnimalSoldiers**

# About the Author

Meish Goldish has written more than 200 books for children. He lives in Brooklyn, New York, where the local aquarium celebrated its first birth of a California sea lion in 2010.